Words From My Mind

by

Henry Sanders

Words From My Mind

Copyright © 2016 Henry Sanders
All rights reserved. No part of this book may be used or reproduced without written permission except in the case of brief quotations for articles or reviews. For more information, visit
hoswrites.com

All poems contained in this book are registered with the Library of Congress, Washington DC

ISBN: 0692617434
ISBN-13: 978-0692617434

Published by
HOSWRITES
Florida, USA
hoswrites.com

DEDICATION

This book is dedicated to those of us experiencing life with all of its ups and downs, its smiles and frowns and all the spaces in between. We may have many things that make us different but we all share emotions and life's lessons. If you have ever experienced love, laughter, sadness, happiness, death, disaster, recovery, and other everyday occurrences, then this book is for you. I hope you can find something in which you can relate.

CONTENTS

TITLE	PAGE
Dream These Dreams for Me	1
I Do Have It Good	2
Let Them Fly	3
Life's Risks and Rewards	5
Over the Crest of the Hill	7
The Nature of Our Love	8
My Girl	9
Move On	11
She Left the Door Opened	12
60 Years to Say This	14
Love TKO	16
I'm Better Because of You	17
Produce and You	18
Read the Signs	19
That Shirt	20
I Dreamed About You	21
Take a Chance	22
I'll Do as You Said	23
The Letter	24
That Phone Call	25
A Second Chance	27
You Didn't Come	28
Our Song	29
Bring My Good Night Back	30
If You're the One	31
It Feels Right	32
Denial	33
I Trust My Heart	34
Those of Us You Hurt	36
Token Words	37
Stay	38
Do I Ask For Too Much?	39

CONTENTS

TITLE	PAGE
My Window	40
It's A Start	41
I Wish I Had Known	42
Peaches Remind Me of You	43
Pickles, Peanut Butter, and Cheese	44
The Willow Tree	45
Falling Again	46
It's Me Not You	47
Awareness too Late	48
Lately	49
I'm Not David	50
Reality	51
Distorted Perception	52
Tears	53
Our First Fight	54
Love at First Sight	55
Hiatus From You	56
The Summer of My First Love	57
Your Passion Defines True Love	58
I Think It's Him Not Me	59
Day by Day	60
Us	61
The Book	62
The Deepest Scars	63
It's Hard Getting Over You	64
I Don't See It Anymore	65
Change Happens	66
Mending Time for Mindy (Etheree)	67
Love's Cruel Part (Crystalline)	68
What Love Does	69
Something is Better than Nothing	70
Remembering the Clay Shapers	71

CONTENTS

TITLE	PAGE
Your Photograph	72
Do You Love Me? (Lanturne)	73
Too Smart to Stay (Kimo)	74
I'm Staying Home Tonight	75
The User	76
A Lot of Nothing (List)	77
Deeply Moved (Diminished Hexaverse)	78
Too Fast, Too Soon	79
Now That She Has My Key	80
I Said Yes	81
My Love and My Life	82
Why Am I Sitting Here?	83
Spring Love	84
This Quiet Time With You	85
That's Why I Called	86
Not Too Far Away	87
Go Slow For the Prize	88
I Guess They Were Wrong	89
Reasons	90
I See It Now	91
Smoking Kills	92
The Women of My Life	93
Good Night Mom	95
The Long Road Ahead	96
I'm Just a Guy in a Chair	98
The Hanging Tree	100
When My Flower Died	101
Memories of Grandmother	102
The Rose and the Cactus	103
The Voices	105
I Need to Want It	106
The Old Pear Tree	108

CONTENTS

TITLE	PAGE
I Always Loved You	110
The Times of Summer	111
Narrow, Winding, Country Road	112
My Own Bird	113
If I Could	114
House Cleaning	115
Two People, Two Hearts, Two Paths	116
Writing What I Should Have Said	118
Just So You Will Know	119
Why I Need You in My Life	121
The Light at the End…	122
Dreams in the Sky	123
Time Retreat	124
Reflections	124
The Children	126
He or The Other?	127
Do You Know What I Know?	128
Cure Hate	130
I Didn't Get Dressed Today	131
Try to Understand Us	132
Two Seasons Ago	134
What a Thing to Ask	135
I Imagined You	137
92 Days Without You	138
This is Not Love	139
Change	140
Not Without You	141
When? (Lanturne)	142
Today I Fell in Love	143
Crowd Sadness	144
My Happy Place	145
Just One More Chance	146

CONTENTS

TITLE	PAGE
It Was Positive (Lanturne)	147
Your Touch	148
When You Dream (Crystalline)	149
Looking Ahead	150
Springtime	151
Index	152

There are many different types of poems. A simple web search will confirm that statement. Some poems in this book are listed with their type in parentheses; unfortunately, there may be many different definitions to determine the type of a poem; therefore, the type listed here, in this book, may be different from what you may know to be true. The type listed here in this book is not meant to be absolute.

*My paper
and my pen
translate
words from my mind.*

Words From My Mind

Dream These Dreams for Me

Dream of dreams of summer breeze
with daisies, daffodils and aged trees

dreams of humming birds and enormous clouds
and imagine if you will as they float by.

Dream of dreams of country walks
and back yard follies and neighbors' talk

of nights with the moon fat and high
and of stranger's greetings as they pass by.

Dream of dreams of front porch swings
and rich traditions and antique things

of farms and stores that are family owned
and a cozy country home of our own.

Dream of me always by your side
and of nights that loneliness made you cry

then know in your heart those tears are gone
and that I will never leave you alone.

Dream of dreams with you in my arms
protecting you from all life's harm

of times when you awake and I'll be there
and gently stroking your soft hair.

No more dreams of scary things
that make you wonder in disbelief

and awaken with a heart heavy and worn
just trust your feelings and you will see.

Words From My Mind

I Do Have It Good

When I stop to think about
how good my life has been

I've got my health, family support
and a pretty good mix of friends.

I have my deep belief in GOD
who has led me all my life

and blessed me more than I deserved
and has given me my wonderful wife.

I've seen a lot, some good some bad
I've done some bad things too

but all in all I'm glad to say
I've managed to come through.

So when I'm down and looking blue
and feeling sorry a bit

I stop and reflect on all my life
and I see how good I really have it.

Words From My Mind

Let Them Fly

I see a mother bird at work
to teach her young to fly
she raised them very close to her
and now prepares good-bye

she protects them with her very life
her heart and soul thus exist
to care for and to protect them all
from egg to chick to this

I think how awful she must feel
to see them all fly away
her precious little baby ones
will soon be on their way

out on their own, in the world alone
to decide what's right and wrong
all things she taught important now
as they learn a brand new song

they'll sing of things dear to their hearts
and not what she might want
she's tempted not to let them go
but in her heart she won't

off they go, wind in wings
the world for them to enjoy
it's sad now in her empty nest
with all her little one's gone

but when she sees how well they fly
she knows she did her part
and when they build their nests one day
it will warm her heart

Words From My Mind

**so let them go mother bird
for nature won't delay
you've done your part so let them go
they'll fly back to you one day.**

    Although "Let Them Fly" seems to be talking about birds, it's really about those of us who are parents letting our children grow up. At some point, all you've taught as a parent will be their guide to a life of responsibility and independence. I know it may be easier said than done.

Words From My Mind

Life's Risks and Rewards

Our lives are ruled from day to day
by things that have gone past

the people we've known, the hurt and pain
somehow those seem to last.

We tend to forget or at least minimize
the days that made us smile

and focus on tears that we've shed
and the pain we carry inside.

Then is it fair or right or what
to ignore the warmth we've felt

and forget how it was to smile all day
at the good hand life finally dealt?

Stop and think and ask yourself
what is your goal in life

to be a success and have happiness
and eventually a husband or wife?

All those things come with risk
and unfortunately no guarantee

sometimes the things we want the most
seem they'll never be

but we can improve on our odds
in this gambling game called life

I've heard it said "Big risk big reward"
I've thought about that once or twice

Words From My Mind

and even if I get hurt along the way
every time, I learn and grow

I take from it what I need
and let the rest of it go.

To me, if life gives only little happiness
then I want all I can get.

I would hate to live a long sad life
and not be happy yet

so I take life's chances over and over
different times and places and such

with the hope one day it will pay off
I look for that day very much.

Think about your heart, your hopes, your dreams
the things you really, really would like

and are they worth the risk you'll take
that, only you can decide.

Words From My Mind

Over the Crest of the Hill

With the warm summer breeze blowing through her hair,
lovely she looked as she stood timidly there.

Her eyes were cool and dark but yet warm and bright,
her smooth skin looked soft, as the sun accented her with its light.

She must have known I would look, I would stare,
if she didn't, why would she remain standing there?

Her dress, long, pretty, being tossed by the breeze,
it was sky blue, with straps on her shoulders, no sleeves.

The wind carried her fragrance,
how sweet did it smell,
was it Candid, French perfume, or Channel, I couldn't tell?

I watched as she slowly walked over the crest of a small hill,
walking through a peaceful, quiet and very grassy field.

Never looking back, not even once, not even at me,
she left her scarf where she was standing, by an oak tree,

then she was gone and I was alone, never to see her that way again,
for over the crest of that hill was where the future

touches the present and the past,
and there she solemnly waits, lying in the grass.

Words From My Mind

The Nature of Our Love

When I think of us together, I think of
warm summer nights. I think of cool
raindrops in the springtime. I think of
white soft snow in the winter. I think of
beautiful sunsets in autumn.
I guess you could say our love is
as natural as nature itself. I love you
and I always will.

Words From My Mind

My Girl

I cast my eyes upon her face
at first to be undecided
years have taught the cautious way
and I have learned to abide it.

We talked at first, not too deep
the usual exchange of verses
we engaged in common courtesy to each
it seemed as if we had rehearsed it.

As time together multiplied
no subject was out of bounds
we talked unlike most strangers would
and found our guards coming down.

For some reason, at the time unknown
I felt no need to conceal
usually though, I'm far more reserved
I had scars that had not yet healed.

As faith declared, it turned out to be
we had more in common than not
as we continued to talk it became easy to see
that this girl impressed me a lot.

Now to make this long story short
we fell in love as you probably figured out
and married each other a few months later
just before that year was out.

Words From My Mind

Sometimes I feel a little cheated
for the years before we met
but then I'm thankful because we did
and I feel the best is still to come yet.

I love her more than you can imagine
I know that's hard to believe
but she means the whole world to me
she helps to make me complete.

Words From My Mind

Move On

If I could move on
I would have surely been gone
because I don't like where I am.

I've spent too much time
letting you control my mind
my thoughts of you, haunt me now.

You said you loved me,
adored and needed me,
so why are you with her, now?

I guess I'm to blame,
because you haven't changed,
it took me a while to catch on.

It's you not me,
It never was me,
God give me the strength to move on.

Words From My Mind

She Left the Door Opened

She left the door opened
and I walked in.
I felt it was meant to be.
We had waited, long by then
and I knew how much
she wanted me.
Her silhouette, called to me,
with a voice so seductively sweet.
And my passion,
full grown,
took control of me,
as she smiled and invited me in.
We talked and touched
and then touched some more.
I could feel
every quiver she made.
With much anticipation
and some nervousness,
not knowing
how things would end.
But I can say
with much jubilation
if you don't take a chance,
you cannot win.

Words From My Mind

What we made
was perfect
in every sense of the word.
I went places
and I felt things…
I didn't want to
return to this world.
My life was changed
from that first time,
I've not been the same ever since,
all because,
she left the door opened
and I took a chance
and walked in.

Words From My Mind

60 Years to Say This

him
I want to tell you something, ol' woman
that you probably already know,
don't know why it took so long,
you know I've always been slow.

I want to tell you thanks,
for the life you devoted to me.
I could not have asked for better
you're the perfect one for me.

So many times you put me first
seldom did I deserve that place
and even through my stubborn ways
you kept me in that space.

You gave me joy and laughter,
encouragement and support.
You comforted my frail spirit
when the cold world made it hurt.

You gave me a family
these angels to be proud of,
never let me stop
kept pushing me with your love.

If I were given sixty more years
to add to the sixty I just went through,
it would be an honor for me,
to spend them all with you.

Words From My Mind

her
Ol' man, I've known that all along
and I do know that you're slow
and I feel your love always
even if you don't say so.

The life I gave to honor you
was returned from what you gave me
not a day went by in sixty years
that I didn't know you loved me.

You gave me a home
and you made it safe,
spoiled me more than I deserved,
made this a happy place,

never once made me feel
that I wasn't your top priority
not one time was I ashamed
by something you did to me.

Words From My Mind

Love TKO

I just watched
as the love of my life
walked away.

The one I honestly believed
to be
my true soul mate.

No other feeling
has ever felt
quite the same

and yet I stand
helpless and broken
as my love walks away.

Powerless things
took control
as we both allowed it to be

and now,
all hope is gone
as my love leaves me.

I have learned
so much from this
I won't make these mistakes again

and it will take
a bit of time
before I can stand again.

Words From My Mind

I'm Better Because of You

I was so down on me
I never thought that I could be
happy or in love.

Didn't see why anyone would be
dumb enough to fall for me
and share with me, their love.

I'm glad you did.

Since you've shared your love with me
I've changed the way I look at me
and others see it too.

I'm gleaming now and they can see
something wonderful inside of me
it must be, the love I feel for you.

Words From My Mind

Produce and You

I thought about you today
while I was shopping
in the produce section.

I saw big, red, strawberries;
firm, ripe, melons
and peaches that smelled
sooo good.

And the zucchini, oh- my- goodness.

I left the market
before I finished.
I can always go back,
tomorrow.

Words From My Mind

Read the Signs

Do you have any
earthly idea
what you have done
to my senses?

I used to know exactly
where my path
led me
but you have changed all that.

I don't know
which way is up.
I cry and
I'm not at all sure why.

I feel as if
my insides are out
and I'm not sure
what I'm sure of.

I asked my girlfriend Joann
what she thought.
She smiled at first, then laughed.
Girl, you're in love.

Words From My Mind

That Shirt

I started spring cleaning yesterday.
It was the first time I felt
strong enough.

I went to my closet first
because that's where most
of the work will be.

About half way through
my selection of tops,
I saw your shirt.

The one I used to wear
when I was in the mood
to get you in the mood.

Spring cleaning is on hold.
My closet door is shut closed.
I have cried for two days now,
all because of that shirt.

Words From My Mind

I Dreamed About You

I dreamed of you the other night
and thought you here, in bed with me.
I awoke and learned you were not there
and realized, it was a dream.
I tried, in vein, to dream again
but tossed and turned and could not sleep,
got out of my bed of loneliness,
sat in my chair of loneliness,
and I… wrote this.

Words From My Mind

Take a Chance

There's something I want to say to you
but it's hard, this is all new to me.
Control is all that I have left
I rely on me, to protect myself
and I know how distant I must seem.

But I've been torn and ripped apart,
been hurt by those I loved the most,
put all my trust and faith in them,
when you talk of love
I cannot boast.

When you tell me, that you love me
it's not that I don't believe it.
When you hold my hand, touch my skin,
it reminds me of old times when,
the motive, was only what they could get.

I want this to be different.
I want this to work, I do.
I'm tired of being cold and alone.
I have this house; I want a home.
Look past my fears and hang ups too.

In time, I'm sure I'll believe again
but let's go slow at first.
Give me time, be patient, please.
Don't give up, I'm worth it, you'll see.
Being alone has created this love thirst.

Now that I opened my heart to you
and admitted more than I had planned.
Where do we go next, from here?
Will you decide based on, love or fear?
I hope you decide to take a chance,

I did.

Words From My Mind

I'll Do as You Said

I saw you yesterday
but you didn't see me.
You were walking down the street,
on Market, heading East.
You had on those dark blue pants,
you know, the one's I bought for you.
The one's I said look good on you.
I wanted to call out to you,
to get your attention,
to let you see me somehow.
But I didn't.
I'm sorry I didn't.
I want you to read this too
but you won't,
because I'll never give it to you.
I have to do exactly what you told me to do.
Move on, forget about us.
Move on, forget about you.
Move on.

Moving on can be the hardest thing to do but not moving on when it's time, can make matters even worse.

Words From My Mind

The Letter

I keep the last letter,
that my old lover gave to me,
tucked away in a small pocket
on the inside of my purse.

I need it fewer these days
than I have in the past,
I've moved ahead a little ways.
I cried a lot at first.

I guess I thought
in some strange way
that as long as I had his words
his feelings would never change.

But my heart did grow stronger,
as I spent more time alone
and the words he left on the page
would only bring me pain.

I keep it now to remind myself
of how far from him I've come
and I read it only seldom now
to remind me of what I've learned.

Words From My Mind

That Phone Call

I answered your cell phone
the other night,
the night you said
you worked late.

The girl who called
sounded distraught and hurt,
said she needed to speak with you,
it was urgent and could not wait.

I didn't ask her who she was.
I could hear passion in her voice.
I felt her sorrow through the phone.
She sounded helpless, hopeless, and lost.

I ended the call, didn't say too much,
broke down and I started to cry.
For the first time since being your wife,
I felt our life was a lie.

I don't know what she means to you
but you, to me, seem to be her world.
I don't know what I mean to you
but I won't be the pathetic other girl.

Words From My Mind

That phone call,
in the middle of the night,
has changed things for sure, for the three of us
and has darkened my light.

I won't make threats
or tell you what to do
but you have a decision
you must make.

I won't make life easy for you.
I can forgive but won't forget.
Think long and hard before you speak.
Don't make a decision you'll regret.

Words From My Mind

A Second Chance

The days ahead
encourage and excite me.
They promise of
things to come
that I have longed to see;

clear blue skies
not much chance of rain.
Long walks
deep and meaningful talks
faint reminders of past pain.

I will try to be for you
what I think you'll be
for me;
a chance to smile again,
a chance to love again--

a second chance.

Words From My Mind

You Didn't Come

I've heard your words,
I've felt your lies,
been held captive by your smile
and bought your promises.

I wear the scars
from your cold touch, from your lies,
from your lack of love for me
and I have cried.

I gave you things
not received in return,
waited for your love,
it didn't come.

I've found a way
to let you go,
it came just in time,
when you didn't come.

Words From My Mind

Our Song

him
Just as I drove into the garage,
the radio played our song,
a flood of memories came to mind
as I sat and sang along.
I remembered the moment
we claimed that tune,
and decided it spoke about us
and vowed to nurture what we had
as fate developed us.
I smiled as I remembered,
the first time that we kissed
and registered the taste of your lips
and recalled as I thought to myself
Wow! I could really get used to this.
I fell in love all over again
and thought how lucky I am.

her
Just as I got into my car
to begin the long trip home,
I turned on the radio
and what I heard was our song.
In an instant, I was back again,
to another place and time.
You still take my breath away,
you melt me every time.
I will never forget your taste,
after our first kiss
and thinking over and over again,
Wow! how sweet is this?
I love you more each passing day
how lucky in love I am.

Words From My Mind

Bring My Good Night Back

I tossed and turned all night
last night,
felt uncomfortable
in my own bed.

Closed my eyes
but could not sleep
watched some
late night TV instead.

No great mystery
I guess or suppose,
for why last night
bothered me so.

I went to bed without you,
a cold and empty place.
I shall not sleep for days to come,
until you are back from that place.

Come quickly to me and grace my bed.
Hold me tenderly once again,
reassure the insecure me,
make me comfortable in my own bed.

Words From My Mind

If You're the One

Day by day,
a little at a time,
you take over my heart.

You came to me,
as a fantasy
and claimed the most bruised part.

You've offered me
a different life
one, I have only dreamed of

and affirmed for me
there is love for me
more than I think I deserve.

I will follow you,
if only for a while,
'cause long term scares me a bit

but if you're the one,
the long awaited one,
my hang ups won't make you quit.

Words From My Mind

It Feels Right

You took a piece of my heart
the first day you smiled at me
and since that day I saw you smile
I've given you much of me.

I have never before, felt so alive
as I do now, when you're with me.
I found the thing I've search for most.
I've found someone who loves me.

Take my heart, I give it to you.
I trust your eyes, your smile.
Handle me with gentleness
let's learn what love's about.

Words From My Mind

Denial

The day you left
I cried and cried
didn't think
I would make it on my own;

didn't fully understand
what went wrong,
all that I knew
is you were gone.

Did it dawn on you
that you crushed me,
that you were to me
more than the air I breathe?

When will you, stop this game,
this game you play with my heart
and come back home, back home to me
where you and I both know you belong?

Refusing to accept or believe something, doesn't mean it's not true. Often times not accepting the truth only adds to your problems.

Words From My Mind

I Trust My Heart

Hold my hand
if you are afraid
even close your eyes
in the midst of a storm.

I will guide you
along your way
and make sure
you are safe and warm.

I can see
the evidence of pain
and things
the others have done.

I'll be sure
not to carry you fast
you'll learn I am
an old fashioned one.

I will help you grow
at your own pace
and cover the earth
if you should fall

and give to you
all that I have
just to help you
become confident and strong.

Words From My Mind

Trust these words
that I impart to you
no ill motive
or hidden purpose do I own.

I just love you
always have,
and following my heart
can't be wrong.

Words From My Mind

Those of Us You Hurt

How could you betray my trust
and do this thing to me?
How could you break my heart
and do this thing to us?

How did it feel to end our life
the one we worked to build
to go against the vows you made,
answer me! I want to know; how does it feel?

I'm crushed, humiliated, through.
I cannot remain here.
I don't know what I'll do
but I cannot decide it here.

I can't even look at you,
you're pathetic, no, you're worse.
I'm not the only victim here
there are others you have hurt.

So in your shame and dark despair,
I hope you realize…
and every time you close your eyes
I hope you hear their cries.

Words From My Mind

Token Words

I pay tribute to you
in these words, I write.
I owe you so very much
for what you have added to my life.
I have never known
the love you carry inside
and the way I still get butterflies
whenever your hands touch mine.
Your eyes melt me
as your passion amazes me
and your love for me
makes me weak.
Sometimes I sit in our soft lamp light
and watch you as you sleep.
Your beauty, in and out, overwhelms me.
I can't go too long
without hearing your voice
which comforts and reassures me.
Thank you for what you've given me
and take these words I write
as a small token from me,
for what your love means to me.

Words From My Mind

Stay

I heard a whisper in my ear
even felt a breath.
I quickly turned to see your face
but all was there was empty space.

My mind plays tricks on my heart,
cruel sometimes, I suppose,
just goes to show how I miss you
and what a lonely heart will do.

I wait for you to rescue me,
my knight with gleaming sword
and take me to our fairytale
where your lips will break this spell.

This spell of loneliness and despair
that captured me while you were gone
but made me love you even more
come heal this heart that you left sore.

Bring back to me my smile and joy,
the things I love and missed the most
and stay with me until the end
and never hurt my heart again.

Words From My Mind

Do I Ask For Too Much?

Call me when you think of me
tell me what's on your mind
don't be afraid to connect with me
tell me how much you're into me
infuse your heart with mine.

Pour your love all over me
drown me with your dreams
share your deepest thoughts with me
learn to put your trust in me
say what you really mean.

If you need your space from me
just go ahead and say it
don't play some silly game with me
where you end up hurting me
are you ready to commit?

Take my hand and comfort me
reassure me when I doubt
don't forget to romance me
from time to time, dance with me
let me check this over, to see what I left out.

Oh! Never, ever, cheat on me
there's only room for us two
and if you say you're in love with me
I'll look for you to show me
that's what true lovers do.

Now that you have heard from me
what do you have to say?
Have you changed your view of me?
Is there still a chance for me?
I hope that you will stay.

Words From My Mind

My Window

As I look out my window
my life takes center stage.
The many things that I have seen
and the many sunny days.

I remember my first day at school,
my first new shinny bike.
The day I broke up with my first love,
I cried and cried and cried.

I remember where I was
the day that Elvis died
and I remember our president
when he went on TV and lied.

This window of mine
has seen a lot
and it keeps me in touch
with who I used to be

and since I'm confined
to this place
I use it
to help me see.

Words From My Mind

It's A Start

These days I have, much time to think.
My solitude enhances my reflection.
Events long gone, now rush back.
I relive each moment, each sensation.

Past loves I've known and cried about,
some good and some not so good at all.
Some bridges I've burned along the way
and the times I promised I would call.

I apologize to all I have hurt.
Back then my only concern was me.
Now I have a new outlook on life
and I realize it's not just about me.

I hope it's not too late
to set my many wrongs right
and move beyond where I am.
I've got better things in my sights.

Words From My Mind

I Wish I Had Known

Yesterday was bad for me,
a year ago on my own.
The things you left
still where they were,
I can't believe you're
really gone.

I tell myself I will be fine,
the clock will heal all my wounds.
I sit some nights with heavy heart
and wish I could tell you how I feel.
I still cry. Is that wrong?
I pray my peace will come soon.

I love you more than I thought I did.
Didn't think I had that much.
My heart now beats one beat less
because that beat belongs to you.
I'd give my all to have you back
I wish I had known, I had that much.

Words From My Mind

Peaches Remind Me of You

Whenever I see peaches
I think of you,

not because
they are so sweet,
not even because
they are so soft.

It's not because
of the fragrance
they give, although,
it could be.

The reason peaches
make me think of you

is because
you love them so
and because
I so love you.

Words From My Mind

Pickles, Peanut Butter, and Cheese

I choose this time,
this place,
this way,
to give you the news
I got yesterday.

I love you so much
you know I do,
our lives are about to change
since now I'm
eating for two.

Words From My Mind

The Willow Tree

In my back yard
in late afternoon
the hottest time of the year,
I find the peace
that my soul needs
under the willow tree.

It provides for me
the things I need
its curtain that touches
the ground
gives to me my privacy
and the birds give me their sounds.

I think of things
important to me
many decisions
I must make
and through the years I've decided a lot
right here in my weeping willow space.

Words From My Mind

Falling Again

**Catch me as I fall.
Be the net that protects me.
Please don't be
another trap for me
like the others that have let me fall
and didn't catch me.
Maybe I am naïve
to think each fall won't be
another painful one
and that your net is secure
and will be the one
that will finally protect me
so that I can heal
and smile again.**

Falling in love can be a double edged sword. On the one side, who doesn't want to be in love, (with the right person)? On the other side, falling in and being in love can leave one vulnerable; and that can be a very scary place to be. But when it's right, it's worth it.

Words From My Mind

It's Me Not You

It's not fair
and I know it,
for me to give you
signals that are
crossed and mixed.
But I too am confused
and don't know where I'm going.
My world has suffered
a terrible blow
that has shaken my foundation
and left me disoriented
and confused and scared.
I won't do to you
the same evil that has
befallen me.
I'm not that bad; yet.
I hope you can see
that my intent is to be
honest and up front with you.
Enough hurt has been done
and I don't want to hurt you.
Maybe in time, a healing away,
things will be different than
the hurt today.

Is it fair that every new partner has to pay the price for all the mistakes of the old partners? No, it's not fair but it's reality.

Words From My Mind

Awareness too Late

Where did you go
and when did you leave?
I just now noticed
you're gone.

I've been busy
these last few years
I'm sorry
I left you alone.

I thought I was doing
what was best for us,
trying to secure
our twilight years.

My focus, I now realize,
was too far off
and I missed
the most important years.

Words From My Mind

Lately

I'm not much surprised
by what you say.
I've heard it all, from you--
lately.

I've come to accept
what I have seen,
things I never would have imagined--
lately.

I find myself doing things
I never thought capable to do
and I think it's all related to
what we've been going through--
lately.

All I know, is,
something has to change,
a new direction, a new start,
something far from this,
'cause I don't like whom I've become
and what my thoughts have been--
lately.

Words From My Mind

I'm Not David

If I had to rate
this night,
...one to ten,
ten being the best,
I would have given it
at least a nine.
Not because
it really wasn't a ten
but because perfection scares me.
But then, all of a sudden,
from so far away
I could not have seen it coming.
She called me
David.

A simple slip-up or a bad sign?

Words From My Mind

Reality

Yesterday it was confirmed;
what I have felt for days.
Things I know are about to change
in so many different ways.

Until this time in my life
I've thought pretty much of me.
My mom and dad would always say
it wasn't always about me.

And now I hear what I didn't then,
it makes more sense to me.
Soon instead of my own way,
it's about the baby in me.

Words From My Mind

Distorted Perception

When I look into the looking glass
it's hard for me so I look fast.
I never like the me I see.
I always see too much of me.

Those I know want me to stop
but they don't feel this pain I've got.
They see outside and then look in.
What makes them say, I'm much too thin?

The things I love, have lost their taste.
It's just as well, I should lose more weight.
Now they say, that I might die.
If they love me, why do they lie?

Mirror, mirror on the wall,
who's the thinnest one of all?
It sure aint me, I'm still too fat,
so I won't eat…and that, is that.

Anorexia is a serious condition and should be treated by medical professionals.

Words From My Mind

Tears

**Tears,
wet release.
They wash away
my pain and grief,
so I can love again.**

Words From My Mind

Our First Fight

Do you realize
we haven't spoken
to each other
all week long?

This can never
happen to us
like this again.
Promise me, please.

Say it won't.
Hold me tight.
Don't let go.
I love you.

Words From My Mind

Love at First Sight

I saw
you move towards me
and I could hardly breathe.
Your beauty captivated me.
I could not move nor could I even speak.
When you stopped and shared your kind words,
I fell in love with you.
I'm glad you stopped
for me.

Words From My Mind

Hiatus From You

I feel the raindrops
on my face
and they help to cool
this hot summer's day
in this smoldering southern place.

The mood is calm,
the pace is slow,
too hot to get excited about much
with clothes sticking to your sweaty skin
but at least everyone says hello.

I came down here
to sort some things through,
no idea how long it will take
and I'm not all too sure
I'm strong enough to move past you.

But I have to consider
all the possibilities--
each time before
I just rushed things on for you.
This time, I need to think about me.

Words From My Mind

The Summer of My First Love

I sit here where sand meets sea
and I think fondly of you and me

and how I felt that summer's day
before you went away.

You were my first, my true love.
You showed me a world I had not known.

And gave to me sweet memories of
the summer of my first love.

Little did I know the lasting of
the things we both enjoyed

and when I yield to the memory of
that restless teenage boy

I pause a bit from fond delight
and imagine what could have been

but then I think of my life now
and all that I've come to enjoy

and how that summer changed my life
by knowing that restless boy.

Words From My Mind

Your Passion Defines True Love

The fullness of your heart
the fullness of your lips
the fullness of your frame
especially your hips.

The softness of your voice
the softness of your touch
the softness of your ways
is why I love you so much.

The honesty of your smile
the honesty of your speech
the honesty of your character
they all have captured me.

The passion in your ways
the passion in your love
the passion that you show for us
defines the phrase "true love."

Words From My Mind

I Think It's Him, Not Me

If I go in there
I know how it will go.
As soon as my feet
touch the floor.

He'll start with me,
start yelling at me,
getting rough with me,
just like the times before.

I used to think it was my fault,
all the things he did to me.
I used to think I deserve it.
I used to think he loves me

but not anymore.
oh no, not anymore.
I think it's him not me.
And I won't be convinced it's me.

If I step through that door,
then I give him the power over me,
power that belongs to me.
Why was that so hard to see?

There's nothing in there
that I cannot replace
or at least come back to get
on my terms. My way.

Words From My Mind

Day by Day

I've put away most foolish things,
that were in contempt of my life,
things that sought to devour me,
and make me their sacrifice.

A new day has dawned and empowered me.
36 days clean and free.
I look back only to guide my way
the horror of my past still haunts me.

I take it slowly these last days.
I try to enjoy what the clock gives me.
I know this is my last second chance.
Life has been more than fair with me.

51 days clean and free.
This is my new personal best.
This is all new and a bit scary to me.
But I cannot quit, not yet.

Today was a bad day,
it nearly caught me off guard,
it brought my past back to me.
I made it through but it was hard.

How much more of this can I take?
It's getting harder as I continue my way.
78 days clean and free.
But tomorrow is still my first day.

Words From My Mind

Us

Now that this is behind us
can we focus on a better us?
It will take the both of us
as we forge our path ahead.

This has tested the love of us.
We evaluated the worth of us...
decided we wanted the both of us
as we forge our path ahead.

I've learned about the strength of us
and I'm sorry for the pain of us.
I'll strive to fix the break of us
as we forge our path ahead.

I'm proud to be a part of us
and I renew my vow to the life of us.
Thank you for another chance for us
as we forge our path ahead.

Words From My Mind

The Book

As I flip the pages
I'm transformed
to another place
another time--

when the sun
seems brighter
than it does now
but I know it's all in my mind.

Thank God for memories,
for they do hold the key
and help make sense
of non-sense things.

I do miss those days,
those good old,
long gone days.
And I long for the joy they bring.

So I'll keep this book
close to my lonely heart
and flip through my past
every now and then.

And enjoy my memories--
my sweet, happy, memories
for I know that they will,
help me smile again.

Words From My Mind

The Deepest Scars

The times that I remember most
are the ones with no specific sway,
instead we followed behind the day.
Back then he was the perfect host
and I think of him often this time of year.

I still have those toys he made,
funny the things I've held on too.
It's hard to explain the things I do.
And I still follow the advice he gave,
times like these I wish he was here.

It's taken me years to get this far.
My therapist said I'm not the norm
most he's known, beat their storms.
But mine I guess, was the deepest scar
and I really wish he were here.

I'll say so long to you again
and wait to see you months from now.
I'll struggle on, some way some how
as I try to move past this pain
and I'll come again next year.

The trauma of a loss can be the most difficult event for some to deal with. Recovery takes time and everyone is different.

Words From My Mind

It's Hard Getting Over You

It was your decision
to leave
and it was my decision
to let you go.

Things had gotten to
an ugly point
and one of us
had to go.

But you've rebounded
well, I see.
The break-up was
good for you.

But I still struggle
with what we lost.
I miss what I had
with you.

In time I'm sure
I'll heal,
they say wounds
always do.

I'm trying hard
to move forward
but it's hard
getting over you.

Words From My Mind

I Don't See It Anymore

When I look at you lately
I don't see
what I used to see
when I could see me with you
and you with me.

Now the thing that
I most see
is the sight of you
in the absence
of me.

Words From My Mind

Change Happens

One-day life hands you a rose
and all is right with the world,

the thorns have been removed
the perfect stem all smooth.

The fragrance and the color
brings joy to others

as they enjoy your rose
in your perfect world.

Then, from nowhere, it comes,
a halt to life's fun.

That perfect rose is no more.
The pain and hurt in store

your life is torn into.
No more perfect world for you.

Isn't it scary how quickly things change
and how life gets rearranged?

Words From My Mind

Mending Time for Mindy (Etheree)

Stop.
No more.
Yesterday
was your last time.
I won't bow to you.
I will set my own rules.
You no longer control me.
I have just liberated me.
Get out of my way, I'm leaving you.
I should have left, way before you broke me.

Words From My Mind

Love's Cruel Part (Crystalline)

It breaks my heart, that I must leave.
I have no answer, for love's cruel part.

Words From My Mind

What Love Does

**Love
forgives pain
caused by hatred
that saddens the soul.
Love.**

Words From My Mind

Something is Better than Nothing

Moments of pleasure
are far and few
but I gladly take
what I can get.

The effects of this
have left me blue
how much worse
can it get?

Wait! Don't answer that,
I don't want to know.
I'm ill prepared
to hear the truth.

I'll keep my head buried deep
and gladly take
all that I can get
of you.

Words From My Mind

Remembering the Clay Shapers

I went back
to my place of birth
for I retain a fondness of,
the air and earth
that greeted me first
and my succor
first love.
I felt the presence
of those who reared
and shaped with patience as with
raw clay
and molded and fitted
with contortionist hands
the sculpture I am today.
I smiled as I
could sense their joy
and cried to feel their pain.
I seldom visit
this incomparable place,
its effects have
left me strained.
But I will keep
this subliminal,
perhaps for another day,
and return here then
to visit again,
the ones who shaped this clay.

Words From My Mind

Your Photograph

This photo I have
that I took of you
these last few months
has rescued me.

I rely on it
to get me through
the toughest times
I've ever seen.

As long as I
can see your face
no harm
will come to me.

It won't be long
and I'll be home
and this war
will go on without me.

A soldier's motivation to return home to his loved one.

Words From My Mind

Do You Love Me? (Lanturne)

**Leave
before
I ask you
to lie to me.
Go!**

It's better to know the sad truth than to be fooled by and live with a good lie.

Words From My Mind

Too Smart to Stay (Kimo)

**After all the pain he has put me through
I would be stupid to stay
life has made me smarter.**

Words From My Mind

I'm Staying Home Tonight

I stayed home tonight
'cause I'm too tired
to go out;
tired of the same ol' thing.
Tired of the same ol' crowd.
The ones with nothing,
trying to get something,
for free.
Not from me. Not tonight.
Tired of being pinched,
pushed, poked and prodded.
I'm not a piece of meat...
not tonight.
I'm tired of the same ol' songs
and the sad stories I hear
in between.
Don't wanna smell
no cheap cologne
or no bad breath, or no new lies.
Not tonight.
I'm staying home.

Words From My Mind

The User

**Must
you go
so soon after?
Will you stay here?
Please?**

Words From My Mind

A Lot of Nothing

One hundred ninety-two pairs of shoes.
Sixty-three outfits.
Twelve tennis bracelets.
Eleven amazing cruises.
Eight rings of precious stones.
Seven unforgettable birthdays.
Three other women.
Two broken hearts.
One lonely woman with all these things…and
no one to love.

Words From My Mind

Deeply Moved (Diminished Hexaverse)

Come with me, my sweet,
trust that I will lead.
Bring your heart with you,
with it you will see,
things your eyes can't see.

I'll show to you,
through gentle touch,
the strength I own
from deep inside.

You will know
from now on,
what it means,

to be
deeply,

moved.

Words From My Mind

Too Fast, Too Soon

I left my past far behind
intent on better tomorrows.
I must search until I find
a solution for all my sorrows.

People I've known throughout the years
let selfish acts define them,
whisper sweet things in my ears
and later, I can't find them.

My heart's been crushed a thousand times,
you would think that I'd know better
but confusion clouds my love sick mind,
it's my fault, because I always let her.

This time it will be different
I refuse to fall too fast.
She's not like the others, she's different.
This time I think we'll last.

Is this real or more of the same old thing?

Words From My Mind

Now That She Has My Key

What was I thinking?
Why did I give her the key
to drive me?

I don't even know
whether or not
she can even drive, me.

Will she drive too fast
and crash and burn,
like the sun burns my skin?

Will she rev up my engine
while I'm standing still
not going anywhere, wasting time, and energy?

What will she do to me
now that I've given her
the key to me?

Why am I always doing this
where did I get the need
to be driven by bad drivers?

But I gave her
the key, to me,
I'll just have to wait and see,

how she drives me.

Words From My Mind

I Said Yes

He has been asking me
for a long time, now
and today, I finally
said yes.
He asked the way
he always does
it was as if
he didn't think I would
say yes.
He should have known.
I showed him the signs.
I thought I had been
very clear,
goes to show how different we are
and how different we really think
but after today,
no doubts remain.
"Are you leaving me?" He asked.
And today, I finally
said yes.

Words From My Mind

My Love and My Life

I know that I can't sing
but when I think of us
I think I can

change the world and me
in it because of you
and the love you show

to me every day we share excites me
and pushes me through because
at the end of the day you are there

making everything right
is your talent, your purpose
and you're what I need

in my life there are few
joys and absolutes
and you are both

my joy and my absolute
my energy and my power
my love and my life.

Everything.

Words From My Mind

Why Am I Sitting Here?

Why am I sitting here
watching movie after movie
of women crying, shopping, talking,
man bashing, rising, falling,
dressing, enabling, settling,
succeeding, failing, cooking,
cleaning, giving, receiving, not receiving,

watching you cry with them,
complain about them, agree with them,
disagree with them, support them,
understand them?
It's because I love you
and I understand you,
like you understand them.

Words From My Mind

Spring Love

It's growing season,
things in bloom.
Birds are nesting
with delightful tune.
Days are long and hot and full,
of activity and purpose and change.
I too am changing
because of you.
My heart is being tugged
and challenged and pulled
in your direction,
growing closer to you
as I find myself,
falling, in love, with you.

Words From My Mind

This Quiet Time With You

It's raining outside
it has been all day.
I guess I should be sad
but I am not.

The sun has gone away,
left the sky without its light.
I guess I should cry
but I will not.

Gloomy are these days
waiting for Spring.
I guess I should be impatient
but I am not.

Soon the sun will come again
and share its warmth, its light.
I guess I should enjoy
this quiet time with you.

Words From My Mind

That's Why I Called

I saw an old friend today
I haven't seen in years.
She still looks great
like she always did.

Time has been really good to her,
married, with kids.
Perfect job, fancy car,
big rings and shiny things

but her eyes did not glow.
They seemed sad and hurt,
holding back the emotions
created by a broken heart.

She said she was going through some things.
Her marriage was in poor health.
The love of her life
no longer wanted her for his wife.

She started to cry
and said she was late
and that she
had to go.

I got in my car
sat there for a moment
I felt bad for her
and thought of us.

I thought back on our life
and how much in love we are,
I felt so close to you
and that's why I called.

Words From My Mind

Not Too Far Away

Chicago never seemed as far
as it feels to me right now.
I know that it's because
my heart is there
and I am here.
The miles and time will teach us
the meaning of many things,
patience, devotion, commitment,
those are the essential things.
Soon this will be behind us
and our eyes will look ahead
and this, that now taunts us
will have strengthened us instead.
So-- wait with me until a time,
not too far from today,
when again, we're together again,
not too far away.

Words From My Mind

Go Slow for the Prize

Things are moving kind of fast,
a little too fast, I think, for me.
Where's the romance,
where's the chase?
I'm not ready to be caught,
at least not yet.
Before you discover
my hidden delights, my treasures,
my prizes, my power,
show me you're worthy
of what you seek.
Don't proceed with the intent
to devour.
Flowers, dinner, movies, talk,
things a sore heart wants to feel.
Invest in me. Put my needs high,
your dividends will be worth it,
you'll see.
So, slow a bit, be patient, wait.
Let's see with our hearts not with our eyes
and let's have fun on this trip we take
and maybe we'll both enjoy the prize.

Words From My Mind

I Guess They Were Wrong

I walked passed a store today,
it had a sad window that looked empty
and lacked life.

I took a chance and took a glance
and I saw there, standing, us two;

walking hand in hand,
just like we used to do.

I had not felt that way
for quite some time.

I stopped, to take it all in.
I thought of a happy time.

You, me and the choices we made,
I started to cry. I still miss you.

It's been nearly two years.
They all said I would have healed.
I guess they were wrong.

Words From My Mind

Reasons

Everything happens for a reason
at least that's what
I've been told.

So when my life
was turned upside down
by someone who didn't even know me,

when the one I adored
was murdered
in cold blood, right there in front of me.

What was the reason for that?

Words From My Mind

I See It Now

Now I see it.
It was there all along
but now I finally see it.

How could it have gone on
so long?
Others told me that they saw it.

I see it now.
Part of me wishes I didn't
but I see it.

Now that I see it,
you have to leave.
Goodbye.

Words From My Mind

Smoking Kills

**Smoking kills,
I promise you it will…
Sooner or later
you'll be dead!
Then what?**

Words From My Mind

The Women of My Life

The women of my life
both now and then,

My wife, my Daughters, my Grandmothers,
my Mothers, Sisters, Aunts, nieces and kin.

Women who have shaped me and molded me into who
I am.

The women of my life both strong and soft,
with touches of soft caress and a firm hand.

Women who have shown me what life has in store,
who taught me and nurtured me and convinced me I
can.
Women who speak from their heart in all sorts of
ways.

All shapes and sizes both short and tall,
there are cookers, sewers, teachers, and leaders,
all textures and tones they represent it all
there are criers, loud talkers, doers and pleasers.

Women of character, passion, commitment and
strength.

Some were taught by the system and did quite well,
some were graduates of the school of hard life.

Some worked in suits and pumps with designer bags,
some wore the scars from a life of trouble and strife.

Women who were determined, focused, guided and
right.

I feel the spirit of the ones who are asleep,

Words From My Mind

and hear the whispers of the ones who are still here.

I miss the ones who left me alone,
and I hold tight to the ones who are still near.

Women of pride, and beauty, with self-respect.

I love them all, who were and still are,
I thank them all for what they gave.

To let me look inside their souls,
and relive all those precious days.

The man I am whether good or not
comes from many places and things in my life

what I've seen and done and have learned from,
but most of all, who I am is because of the women of
my life.

Words From My Mind

Good Night Mom

I remember days with my mom
when all was right with the world.
She would comfort my childhood woes
and called me her pretty girl.

We would do all there was
together, just us two.
We'd cook and talk and laugh out loud,
and she told me what boys would do.

Nothing was too complicated
for her wisdom to work through.
She said she had high hopes for me
no matter what I chose to do.

She lifted me when I was down,
and sent me on my way.
She gave me things that I still own
and cherish to this day.

I place these flowers by your side,
the ones you always liked.
I kiss your head and your lips,
good night my heart, good night.

Words From My Mind

The Long Road Ahead

For years I've spent much of my time
thinking of the pain you've caused

the power I gave to make you strong
and how I put my dreams on pause

the things I wanted were all for you
your happiness was my life's chore

it's hard to reflect on those yesterdays
my spirits are still bruised and sore

I know you love me but that's not enough
apologies grow weak over use

I accept what you are, your problems and such
but I refuse to stay weak from abuse

you've been, for years, part of the problem
the reason I had to endure

I forgive you for your treatment of me
now do your part for the cure

we both need to heal and move on
our past can't stand in our way

we have to forgive and try to forget
and make growth the order of the day

I should hate you, you're right, I know
but I've moved far beyond hate

I've placed myself on a higher plane
a place where there's no room for hate

Words From My Mind

seek forgiveness from Him first
then you will have begun

make right to me, all your wrongs
start with the most painful ones

we will reach our goal one day
the road long and hard, ahead

talking is key to resolution
because now I'm no longer afraid.

Words From My Mind

I'm Just a Guy in a Chair

To sit has become my destiny
my freedom of choice, stripped from me
the road ahead, one of recovery
as I evaluate my new life.

Bound to this chair by circumstance
never to enjoy another dance
a victim of pity and curious glance
as society passes me by.

For a time, I asked the question why?
I was honest, smart, had a good life
a beautiful, devoted and sensuous wife
but that's in question now.

I fear for things I cannot change
my routine has now been rearranged
my limbs are dead but cause me pain
my mind has suffered the most.

Each day is new and it challenges me
to overcome that which over comes me
to take back my life that was taken from me
I must find a way to endure.

I am not defined by this chair
it's just a device to get me there
I understand why you stand and stare
but take the time to know me.

Words From My Mind

Inside I'm still the same old guy
I have the same determined drive
just like you, I'm glad to be alive
we're more the same, you and me.

Look past this chair I'm sitting in
see the person that's within
there's a good chance we could be friends
I'm just a guy in a chair.

Words From My Mind

The Hanging Tree

I have seen it many times from off a ways,
both as the sun goes and comes,

I have watched as strong winds came
through seasons and months and days,

in it, I've seen birds build nests to lay their eggs,
and squirrels and raccoons play.

I saw some folk at a picnic one day,
before the rain came.

I once heard fruit would grow so great
the limbs would bend and lean.

The way it sat on top the hill
was a sight you shoulda' seen.

The one who planted the seed before,
could not have planned for this,

the tree that adorned the meadow,
to be used and degraded for this.

I knew of many that ended here.
I prayed it would not end here for me.

Words From My Mind

When My Flower Died

Why must flowers die
wither and lose their color?

The beauty they share
should be eternal

they spread so much joy
they warm cold places

they dance in summer breeze
and reach high towards the sky

an inspiration to us all
a challenge to protect and raise

we touch gently, careful not to bruise
they touch lightly but affect us greatly

when they arrive, joy abounds
plans have been made months ago

but when they die
no one is prepared, really

we all feel deprived
cheated, in many ways

I love you my flower
I love you my flower, good-bye.

this is about the death of a child.

Words From My Mind

Memories of Grandmother

Lately my mind has continued to go
back to a time I knew

a time I am quite fond of
where smiles and a warm heart protected me

the hands that reared and loved me
that held and in time, released me

hands that mastered both strength and warmth
I knew nor know no other like them

skies were never gray, only blue
with thick white clouds that looked comfortable

when she was in control, it was my privilege
and she was almost always in control

she gave and gave and then again
and asked for nothing

I accepted all that she gave
and own it till this day

I am indebted with a debt I owe to her
and I feel I can never repay

the memories keep me strong
the laughter rings softly in my ears

nothing lasts forever but I think
that forever for me I will hold on to these memories…

Words From My Mind

The Rose and the Cactus

The Cactus and the Rose
were planted in the same pot

they shared the same soil
near the same spot

watered from the same pail
nourished and nurtured the same way

carefully covered through the night
shared the sun during the day

at first it seemed to go just fine
they even had things alike

they both had thorns in their sides
and flowers that reached for the light

but it wasn't long, before you could see
a very distinct difference about

and not long from their start as one
that one had to be taken out

you see, they started to grow in different ways
couldn't live together in the same pot

their roots that touched in the early years
could no longer share the same spot

Words From My Mind

you could see them slowly dying away
their differences were more now than ever

so they were replanted in different pots
since it was sure they couldn't live together

once they had their own pot and soil
and needs unique to them each, were met

they started to grow and thrive again
and neither Rose or Cactus has stopped yet.

Words From My Mind

The Voices

They have told me this, many times before
but I was strong and I said no
but they would not stop
they just kept on
as I fell hard to the floor

I had no power over their words
their voices would not let go
they outnumbered me three to one
and whatever they said I heard
I heard every word

for a time, I felt in control
that too was short
soon I didn't know
what was real and what was not
before they came I was young, now I feel old

I could not have done this
if I had been alone,
I did not want to do this
but my will is not strong
they marked the spot so I could not miss.

As I lie here, my life slipping away
thinking where I went wrong
how I gave up my power
how with my own hand
I made this my last day.

The perils of mental disease.

Words From My Mind

I Need to Want It

Lies I've told with an untouched heart
hurting those I should not

I see me and I'm not pleased
I try but I always give in

our union is threatened, it has been from the start
now a second small life may slip through my soul

I say I love you, do I?
I've shown you actions that contradict

I see small bright eyes
those from our labor of love

I see dreams we've talked about
I remember plans we've made

I feel the hurt still from the first
I hear words of love from you

a battle within myself
I seem at ease when I'm under the juice

you say you understand me
you share my grief; thanks.

I've asked for chances before
you gave, I abused, I'm sorry.

Words From My Mind

When I look into your eyes
I see what you would like to see in me

I feel fortunate that you care
I just need to want what you want for me.

My crutches are running out
soon I'll have to stand on my own.

I hope you'll be there as you are now
I hope we both can see what you want for me.

Words From My Mind

The Old Pear Tree

In my past deeply engraved in memories fond
I see you, ol' pear tree

standing tall touching the sky
refusing to bow, even to March winds

strong, majestic, with leaves in summer, full and darkest green
carrying heavy your gifts, even if only seldom

under you, ol' pear tree, a cushion, nature made,
waiting there for only me

the shaded kingdom, refuge from the sun
here I would sit, my eyes sometimes closed

often lying supine, looking through your arms
I could see shapes formed by silently passing clouds

I would think about days past
I would plan days to come

you heard a lot from me, ol' pear tree
saying things I dare not otherwise

you were a friend in the deepest sense
never did you judge, betray or give bad advice

you would listen for hours on end
occasionally giving one of your treasures

I felt warm near you, ol' pear tree
even when nature demanded your leaves and forced
your treasures to the ground

Words From My Mind

many years ago since I occupied this, my spot
many words my mouth has spoken since talking to
you, my old friend

I see with a sadden stare
you're not so tall anymore

your leaves are few, nearly none. Your treasure no
longer comes
now you bend to even the slightest breeze

I thought, my friend, you would last forever,
dear old pear tree

I look and somehow I feel that as I needed you
through the years, you also needed me.

Words From My Mind

I Always Loved You

There you were, like a dream dreamt a thousand
times before.
You said nothing; silent and timid you were.

My heart did not skip, the night we met,
my eyes however saw a difference in you.

I had prayed and imagined for so long
could this, I hoped, be my reward?

Qualities that I adore
I soon saw in you.

The feeling I so long hoped for
I soon started to feel with you.

The first time I saw you, wasn't love
the second time was the start.

Ever since the night we kissed
I knew that I always loved you.

Words From My Mind

The Times of Summer

The sky these days, a perfect Carolina blue
with clouds that say things familiar.

The air redolent with the gift from wild flowers,
bees know their way; God saw to that.

The grass is as green as it ever will be,
as the trees stand proud when they touch the sky.

The birds now fly with a different purpose,
carrying things necessary for the next generation.

The sheets dance on the line as gentle breezes blow,
making fresh the bedding for the night.

The yard chores, more pleasurable now,
this took months of patience.

Hearts are warm and the days are long,
these are the times of summer.

Words From My Mind

Narrow, Winding, Country Road

Life unchanged from years ago
it seems the clock stood still

things are simple, peaceful here
the smell of daffodil

around and through, over and beyond
the roads here seem to roam

the mailboxes dart the country side
as warm memories bring me home

one must stop so the other may pass
and conversation to be told

the thing I remember most of all
is a narrow, winding, country road.

Words From My Mind

My Own Bird

If I were a bird
then I too would fly
as the other birds do.
I think however though,
I would probably fly
my own course and speed.

I would not chirp
just to follow suit,
it would be only when
I wanted to sing
and even then if all alone
so be it.

I would not eat
a worm or bug or such,
if my appetite did not say to.
I would not be compelled
by the sparrow or the crow.

And when the winter did come
and I did not want to go,
I don't think
that I would be persuaded
by the flock.

I would build my nest
dependent upon
where I choose to live.

I'm not a bird from the dodo flock
although questionable I know.
I'm only trying to make a point
to the sparrow and the crow.

Often times in life, it's better to fly alone than to get
involved with a bad flock.

Words From My Mind

If I Could

I would gladly move the earth
to stand by your side

I would put your heart in my hand
to protect it from all harm

I would cradle your spirit
to keep you strong

I would tell you sweet words
to show that the world can be kind

I would caress you softly
to make you feel at ease

I would listen to your thoughts
to share your world

if I could be with you now, I would
I would stay with you always, if I could.

Words From My Mind

House Cleaning

Step into my room
and help me clean

open windows; full,
let in the sun and the sweet smells

let me hear the birds sing;
I had forgotten how the birds sing

for a long time, dark curtains have shaded my room
kept what is in from getting out

kept what was out from getting in
too long, dark curtains have shaded my room

come through the door if you dare
are you sure you want this?

Much work lies ahead I know,
work I'm ready to start though.

I won't ask much of you;
understanding, communication, and respect

I ask of you
what I'll give to you.

In time, my room will be bright again
comfortable and functional again.

if you will, will you?
I'm asking you to stay.

Words From My Mind

Two People, Two Hearts, Two Paths

I broke your heart and I know it
but that's the last thing I wanted.

You possess a love deep inside
and a glow that says committed.

When two agree, life is simple
when two disagree, life is not.

I think at first, before we knew,
we felt what we each wanted too.

You, your way and I, mine
we traveled a much different path

I saw in you what I used to want
and in many ways I still want

just not now;
just not now.

As I sit away from you
my heart keeps asking about you.

I miss you,
I really do.

Words From My Mind

I hope through your next door
a room full of love awaits

and sunshine and cactus too
can be yours forever more.

My wish is that somehow, some way
you can find it in your heart

to remember my smile, my touch
and all our talks.

Please don't hate me,
good-bye.

Words From My Mind

Writing What I Should Have Said

There are some things you need to hear
and I am in error for not having said them.

There are some feelings that I should have shared
and all along I should have been showing them.

I have not said nearly often enough
how much of my world you possess.

I take for granted you know all this
but it's good to hear it, never the less.

I love you to the depths of my heart
and want you in my life; always.

You have saved me from my past,
brought sunshine to my once rainy days.

I shiver sometimes when I think about
the bond that has grown between us,

to know that life has in store for us
much more than either one of us has seen.

I look forward to glorious days,
to tears of joy and laughter,

to front porch swings and summer breeze
and all the love we have sought after.

Words From My Mind

Just So You Will Know

I have seen with my own eyes
the joy true love can bring

and I have longed for many years
to feel that very thing

I would see those passersby,
so in love with each other

and think that love had passed me by,
the truth could not be further

I would often think and hope,
one day my pain would end

and feel that special thing called love,
so I could live again

into my life, you walked right in,
as if you knew my needs

took control of my heart
and I began to see

I saw a heart that could nurture and forgive
I saw compassion in your eyes

and for the first time in so many years
my spirit was energized.

Words From My Mind

I said I do; I mean I will--
be there for you always.

You've given me a second chance
to enjoy my future days.

I love you more than I thought I could
and my love for you still grows

and from now on, through the years,
I will tell you, so you will know.

Words From My Mind

Why I Need You in My Life

I need you in my life
to show me the meaning of truth

to make me know the power of laughter
and what trust and commitment are all about.

I need you in my life
for many reasons,

but most of all,
because I love you.

Words From My Mind

The Light at the End...

How long have I waited?
Nearly more days than I can count.

How long has my heart ached?
Night after night with little rest.

How sad are my eyes?
They talk now only in tears.

How go my dreams?
Long and dark through sleepless nights.

What happened to my paradise?
The storm blew in and stayed.

Whatever became of my dreams?
They still are here inside.

Will they ever come to be?
One day, one day...

Words From My Mind

Dreams in the Sky

I reach into the deep blue skies,
to escape the world beneath.

Boundless, endless deep blue skies,
a different experience for each.

The earth below all dreary and low,
the clouds invite my heart.

As smiles float by in the sky,
somber realities take part.

The sky is high above my reach,
the world below is now.

My dream of escape into the sky,
quietly passes me by.

Words From My Mind

Time Retreat

Can it be that when my spirits fall
I ache for the days I once knew

a sunnier time, a younger time
a time when now was so far away

the summers seemed greener
the winters seemed to last on and on forever

my worries flew on the wings of doves
problems of the world did not reach me

scrapes and scratches were common place
but I knew that and did not mind

it seemed happiness was mine most often
the times I cried were far and few in between

then time began to move
more quickly than at first

changes before my eyes
some I did not like

now when time is about to overwhelm me
I take control

I look back and I see
a time when now was so far away.

Words From My Mind

Reflections

Reflection has become more a part of my life
as my life goes by.

I stop to think about simple things,
things, that years ago, didn't catch my eye.

Oh, it's not hard to look and see
a different way to view things.

I see accomplishments made on time
and how many things are still dreams.

All of my reflections are not the same
some are sweet and make me sigh

others come with a measure of pain
and often times I cry.

Either way, the job gets done.
I see things that I need to see.

I change in my life the things I can.
What I cannot change, I let it be.

I like to reflect; it makes me grow.
Over all, I feel pretty good about my life.

I think things became much easier for me
when I learned to take things in stride.

Words From My Mind

The Children

Smiles as bright as summer time
innocent as angels above

saying, doing, without regard
to hang-ups plagued by adults

we watch them play and play along
we hear them laugh and sing

they adapt really well to where they are
they play dress up for who they want to be

life is simple as it should be
carefree and fun for awhile

enjoy these years our little ones
as we did in our own time

nothing on earth is more precious to see
than God's little gifts with a smile.

Words From My Mind

He or The Other?

Why must I evaluate
and pick one over the other

they both have looks and charm
any girl would love to discover.

He, says he loves me
The Other, says I love him.

The Other, says we'll go places.
He, has taken me to them.

He, buys me things I adore
The Other, says after him I don't need anything more.

He, gently holds my hand
The Other, boastfully announces he's my man.

The Other, says he works late so he's seldom at home
He, constantly leaves sweet messages on my phone.

He, lets me drive his sporty new wheels
The Other, says driving is really no big deal.

He, doesn't pressure me and says we can wait
The Other, can't keep his hands off me, ever since our first date.

He, says he'll marry me and build me a home
The Other, says why get married and spoil the fun.

Now you can see the dilemma facing me
girls who would you choose, The Other or He?

Words From My Mind

Do You Know What I Know?

The time has come
to move from two

to change our course
and move as one.

Who knew?

Tears will flow
it can't be helped

I won't place blame
but I'll share it with you.

I suspected.

The transition that will come
can be smooth or hard

the choice of which is our own
as we both strengthen our guard.

I believed.

The years that passed were not all bad
some good can come from most anything.

I did not want what has to be
but I don't see any positive change.

I hoped.

Words From My Mind

Love alone is not enough
many things more are needed.

We can both gain strength from this.
we both have begged and pleaded.

I'm sorry our end has come to this,
Good-bye.

Words From My Mind

Cure Hate

The sounds I hear are the sounds of death
the bellows, the screams, the cries
the pain, how grotesque you never felt
as generations of people die

to erase a people from the face of the earth
for no other reason than you can
to rob a mother of her baby's birth
to gain power at the expense of another man

how could a man convince himself
that what he does is justified
no matter the motive he may claim
he still has committed genocide

and how could a world stand and watch
as history writes this horrible scene
to turn away and watch something else
and give permission to a maniacal fiend?

But some did survive and history did record
a lesson for all to appreciate
to do unto others as you want done
and do everything you can to cure hate.

Words From My Mind

I Didn't Get Dressed Today

I found your key
this morning,
as I was getting dressed.

I thought of you.
I thought of us,
and it made me smile.

I remembered,
what we had together,
and I miss you.

I felt, for a moment,
as if you were here
with me, now.

I must admit,
I cried a little.
I'm not healed yet.

I felt a pain
deep inside.
The hurt was real.

I undressed,
got back in bed,
no work today.

It's been two weeks
trying to get dressed
and I cannot.

I miss you.
I love you.
I do.

Words From My Mind

Try to Understand Us

As the sun falls low
behind the afar ridge line
the darkness covers us all
and the light from the lantern leads the way

he comes tonight like many nights before
and he takes a piece of me away
without regard or respect, no thought or care
he takes what he wants and he leaves

and I, left to imagine it all
but the worst does not happen to me
I close my eyes as I know she does
and I wait till she's returned to me

nothing to do but scream inside
for out loud would cause more pain
I learn to endure and minimize it all
Oh God! must I go insane?

The strength of a man
is measured in many ways
by what he can move
and what he allows to move him

each day I get closer to the edge
but she tries to pull me back; safe.
I can't look straight into her eyes anymore
without feeling a generation of hate.

I did not protect as my fathers did
I did not provide her needs
and she has no bounty to speak of
no legacy to be proud to leave

Words From My Mind

how should I feel, when I know,
that my brothers will know?
I will see the outward proof
of what I could not stop

you tell me sir, how does this sound
can you even imagine the life?
To know that this is your lot in life
and this is mother, sister or wife

place your head on my shoulders
see what my father's saw
know that the scars still are deep
and understand this is who we are

give us a chance to heal our hearts
support what we say we need
let us talk and pray and cry
and keep our self-respect

you don't have to apologize
for something you were not responsible for
but show some compassion for
a people who don't want to hurt anymore.

This poem talks about the effects of slavery and how a slave owner (master) would come in the night and take a woman for his pleasure and her husband or brother or father or son, could do nothing about it and the deep hatred this must have caused. And how it may affect generations of people today.

Words From My Mind

Two Seasons Ago

When you moved here last summer
I had a feeling about you
and now two seasons past
I'm glad I had that feeling
about you.
Let's go get some breakfast.

Words From My Mind

What a Thing to Ask

Do I love you?
Why do you ask?

As if to confirm
the sea and the sky.

When did I love you?
I thought you knew.

From the moment your lips
uttered the same.

Why do I love you?
This could take a while,

here goes.

I love you,
for who you are,

with imperfections
in a perfect way,

for your patience with me
when I am off in my own space,

for your forgiveness of me
when I have stepped off the edge,

for your acceptance of me
when I won't come in from the ledge,

for seeing in me
my desire to please you,

for holding me
when my arms are folded,

Words From My Mind

for speaking to me,
with tears in your eyes,

for telling me
you still want to try.

A mystery to me,
your love for me.

I just know that
I am glad it exists,

and I hope you know
that I love you too,

and forgive me
for anything I have missed.

Words From My Mind

I Imagined You

I've never felt hands so strong
or arms that make me safe.
I've never seen eyes like yours
that look into my soul.
I've never tasted lips so sweet
that make me crave for sweets
and I never imagined this happiness
would ever come to me.

Words From My Mind

92 Days Without You

This makes for me
day number 92,
since I've last
spoken with you.

I never thought that I
could go this long
without saying
I love you, to you.

When you walked out
and said I would call
I thought I would give in
like I always do.

But that was not so
I've managed without you.
Oh it's been rough, I know
but it's been 92 days without you.

They say it takes
90 days to be through,
I hope they're right,
it's been 92 days without you.

Words From My Mind

This is Not Love

What kind of love is this you give
if all I do is cry?
If this is what you call love
then I'm calling you a liar.

Words From My Mind

Change

The part of me that I would change
if I could change a part of me
would be the very part of me
that wants to change a part of me.
I need to accept the parts of me
that fit together to make all of me
but there's a little part of me
that wants to change a part of me.

Words From My Mind

Not Without You

A bird cannot sing without the sun
a rose cannot glisten without morning dew

a man cannot live by bread alone
and I cannot live without you.

When? (Lanturne)

**When
did this
raw passion
turn into real
love?**

Words From My Mind

Today I Fell in Love

I have seen you
every day for many days
but never before
as I saw you today.

It wasn't your hair.
It wasn't your clothes,
although when I saw you
I saw you in a different way.

Your smile seemed brighter.
Your eyes seemed warmer.
The words from your lips
sounded sweeter still.

And today, when you touched my hand
for the first time
in all those days
you made my world stand still.

Words From My Mind

Crowd Sadness

Crowds used to make me sad,
because in my mind
they were made of couples;
many couples.
New couples, old couples,
casual ones, serious ones.
Couples in love.
I was not in love.
I was not part of a couple.
That made me sad most of all.

Words From My Mind

My Happy Place

Butterflies and deep blue skies
both remind me of you.
Long evening walks and
deep meaningful talks
are some of the things I
love about you.

Making dreams and chasing dreams
as most of them have come true.
And life is grand for you and me
more so than I'd dreamed it would be.
You came into my broken life
and you completed me.

I feel blessed to be with you,
to share and grow and laugh out loud,
to watch old movies and sleep in late
I love my life I love this space
and this thing between you and me.
And I'm in my most happy place.

Words From My Mind

Just One More Chance

I can almost taste the salt
in the ocean breeze.
And when I do,
it makes me think of you.

You seemed the happiest when
you were being kissed
by the waves
and those were our better days.

Since you've been gone
the sea has lost its power,
at least for me anyway.
I wonder if you feel that way.

One more season.
One more month,
a couple of weeks will do,
just one more chance with you.

Words From My Mind

It Was Positive (Lanturne)

**Warm
glowing
radiant
can't wait to be
mom.**

Words From My Mind

Your Touch

**Your touch
starts my rhythm,
increases my desire,
puts sweet images in my brain.
Thank you.**

Words From My Mind

When You Dream (Crystalline)

**Leave on the light, I want to see
the look you show, when you dream of me.**

Looking Ahead

**Memories
make me
want our
future.**

Words From My Mind

Springtime

**Flowers
fragrant filled
dancing in sequence
as the breeze blows,
sweet.**

INDEX

TITLE	PAGE
60 Years to Say This	14
92 Days Without You	138
A Lot of Nothing (List)	77
A Second Chance	27
Awareness too Late	48
Bring My Good Night Back	30
Change	140
Change Happens	66
Crowd Sadness	144
Cure Hate	130
Day by Day	60
Deeply Moved (Diminished Hexaverse)	78
Denial	33
Distorted Perception	52
Do I Ask For Too Much?	39
Do You Know What I Know?	128
Do You Love Me? (Lanturne)	73
Dream These Dreams for Me	1
Dreams in the Sky	123
Falling Again	46
Go Slow For the Prize	88
Good Night Mom	95
He or The Other?	127
Hiatus From You	56
House Cleaning	115
I Always Loved You	110
I Didn't Get Dressed Today	131
I Do Have It Good	2
I Don't See It Anymore	65
I Dreamed About You	21
I Guess They Were Wrong	89
I Imagined You	137
I Need to Want It	106
I Said Yes	81
I See It Now	91

Words From My Mind

INDEX

TITLE	PAGE
I Think It's Him Not Me	59
I Trust My Heart	34
I Wish I Had Known	42
I'll Do as You Said	23
I'm Better Because of You	17
I'm Just a Guy in a Chair	98
I'm Not David	50
I'm Staying Home Tonight	75
If I Could	114
If You're the One	31
It Feels Right	32
It Was Positive (Lanturne)	147
It's A Start	41
It's Hard Getting Over You	64
It's Me Not You	47
Just One More Chance	146
Just So You Will Know	119
Lately	49
Let Them Fly	3
Life's Risks and Rewards	5
Looking Ahead	150
Love at First Sight	55
Love TKO	16
Love's Cruel Part (Crystalline)	68
Memories of Grandmother	102
Mending Time for Mindy (Etheree)	67
Move On	11
My Girl	9
My Happy Place	145
My Love and My Life	82
My Own Bird	113
My Window	40
Narrow, Winding, Country Road	112
Not Too Far Away	87

Words From My Mind

INDEX

TITLE	PAGE
Not Without You	141
Now That She Has My Key	80
Our First Fight	54
Our Song	29
Over the Crest of the Hill	7
Peaches Remind Me of You	43
Pickles, Peanut Butter, and Cheese	44
Produce and You	18
Read the Signs	19
Reality	51
Reasons	90
Reflections	124
Remembering the Clay Shapers	71
She Left the Door Opened	12
Smoking Kills	92
Something is Better than Nothing	70
Spring Love	84
Springtime	151
Stay	38
Take a Chance	22
Tears	53
That Phone Call	25
That Shirt	20
That's Why I Called	86
The Book	62
The Children	126
The Deepest Scars	63
The Hanging Tree	100
The Letter	24
The Light at the End…	122
The Long Road Ahead	96
The Nature of Our Love	8
The Old Pear Tree	108
The Rose and the Cactus	103

Words From My Mind

INDEX

TITLE	PAGE
The Summer of My First Love	57
The Times of Summer	111
The User	76
The Voices	105
The Willow Tree	45
The Women of My Life	93
This is Not Love	139
This Quiet Time With You	85
Those of Us You Hurt	36
Time Retreat	124
Today I Fell in Love	143
Token Words	37
Too Fast, Too Soon	79
Too Smart to Stay (Kimo)	74
Try to Understand Us	132
Two People, Two Hearts, Two Paths	116
Two Seasons Ago	134
Us	61
What a Thing to Ask	135
What Love Does	69
When My Flower Died	101
When You Dream (Crystalline)	149
When? (Lanturne)	142
Why Am I Sitting Here?	83
Why I Need You in My Life	121
Writing What I Should Have Said	118
You Didn't Come	28
Your Passion Defines True Love	58
Your Photograph	72
Your Touch	148

www.ingramcontent.com/pod-product-compliance
Lightning Source LLC
LaVergne TN
LVHW051101080426
835508LV00019B/2003